COOKING
for
CHRISTMAS

*A Cook's Countdown to
Planning the Perfect Christmas*

Linda Doeser

This edition published in 2010
LOVE FOOD is an imprint of Parragon Books Ltd

Parragon
Queen Street House
4 Queen Street
Bath BA1 1HE, UK

ISBN: 978-1-4454-1408-9

Printed in China

Produced by The Bridgewater Book Company Ltd
Photography by Ian Parsons and David Jordan
Home economy by Richard Green, Brian Wilson and Jacqueline
Bellefontaine

NOTES FOR THE READER

- This book uses imperial and metric measurements. Follow
  the same units of measurement throughout; do not mix
  imperial and metric.

- All spoon measurements are level: teaspoons are assumed to
  be 5 ml, and tablespoons are assumed to be 15 ml.

- Unless otherwise stated, milk is assumed to be whole, eggs
  and individual vegetables such as carrots are medium, and
  pepper is freshly ground black pepper.

- Recipes using raw eggs should be avoided by infants, the
  elderly, pregnant women, convalescents, and anyone
  suffering from an illness.

Contents

INTRODUCTION

Fine food and edible treats are among the most traditional and best-loved aspects of Christmas, especially if you are sharing them with family and friends. For the family cook, however, the whole event can be quite stressful and involve a lot of hard work. This book is designed to make all the preparation and cooking as trouble-free as possible, so that everyone has a really enjoyable time. It is divided into four chapters, to make planning your Christmas entertaining easy.

Even if you usually leave your Christmas shopping until just before Christmas Eve, you will find the recipes in the first chapter, The Festive Season, invaluable for getting a head start on your Christmas catering. You may even decide to make some edible gifts. The recipes allocated to Christmas Eve include many special touches that we often intend to add but never quite get round to. Preparing them on Christmas Eve ensures that they are not overlooked. The third chapter, Christmas Day, is packed with all the traditional favourites to make your Christmas meal a sparkling and memorable occasion, including a fabulous breakfast to help you start the day in style. The last chapter, Boxing Day, offers some ingenious ways with leftovers and some tempting dishes to counterbalance the richness of the Christmas feast, while still maintaining a mood of celebration.

Timing the preparations for the main Christmas meal and the other festive meals can be complicated, so a timetable for each chapter is included in the following pages. These will help you avoid such common hiccups as finding that the potatoes are still rock hard when everything else is ready to be served or suddenly realizing at midnight on Christmas Eve that you have almost forgotten to ice the cake.

GUIDE TO RECIPE KEY

Simplicity

Recipes are graded as easy, very easy or extremely easy.

Preparation time

Where marinating, chilling or cooling are involved, these times have been added on separately: e.g., 15 minutes + 30 minutes to marinate.

Cooking time

Cooking times do not include the cooking of side dishes or accompaniments served with the main dishes.

Number of servings

Recipes generally serve six to eight people. Simply divide proportionately when catering for fewer people.

These timetables won't take the work out of Christmas cooking, but they will make it very much easier to organize. Simply refer to the dishes that you plan to cook yourself for Christmas.

All the eagerly anticipated seasonal delights are here, from Roast Turkey with Bread Sauce to Mulled Wine, Christmas Pudding and Irish Coffee. There are some delicious nibbles and cocktails to serve before the meal, tasty starters, a choice of stuffings to accompany the turkey or goose, even a delicious roast for any vegetarians in the family. As well as familiar favourites such as Mince Pies, there are also some more unusual Christmas specialities such as Sloe Gin.

Take time to browse through the pages before you decide what you want to serve over Christmas this year. Be selective; if you are going to make Orange Rum Butter, you don't need to make Brandy Butter as well. If you're not keen on the traditional Christmas fruitcake, opt for the ever-popular chocolate Yule Log instead.

Enlist the help of the family – everyone can manage to do something, even if it's just rolling Chocolate Truffles in cocoa powder. Get the children to hand out the nibbles and make people take turns in the kitchen clearing up.

Whether you are planning a massive family gathering or just a quiet Christmas for two, you are sure to find the perfect dish, the ideal drink and a self-indulgent treat that will make the day extra special.

Festive Season

Getting part of the main Christmas cooking completed well in advance makes everything so much easier when the great day comes. Some foods actually benefit from being made ahead of time.

COUNTDOWN

SEPTEMBER–OCTOBER
Bottle Sloe Gin (see page 29) to give it time to mature for Christmas.

NOVEMBER
Make the Christmas Cake (see page 17). Fruitcake keeps well and can be made even more delicious by occasionally 'feeding' it with brandy.

Make the Christmas Pudding (see page 14). The traditional date for doing this is 'Stir-up Sunday', the last Sunday before Advent. Follow the custom of letting everyone in the family stir and wish three times.

Check stocks in the drinks cabinet and replenish supplies if necessary.

DECEMBER
Biscuits, snacks and sponge cakes for Christmas Day itself cannot be made very far in advance, although unfilled Brandy Snaps (see page 22) can be stored in an airtight container. The dough for Cheese Straws (see page 30) can also be made in advance and stored in the freezer. Thaw at room temperature before rolling out and baking. Such home-made festive nibbles make a welcome treat for pre-Christmas visitors.

Remember to allow at least 24 hours after covering the Christmas cake with marzipan before icing it. The icing also needs time to set.

Make a list of all the ingredients you will require and plan your shopping carefully. Place any special orders early in the month, but don't buy fresh vegetables or fruit too far in advance. Check the use-by dates on store-cupboard items, such as flour, to avoid any last-minute panics.

TIMETABLES

Christmas Eve

For some, Christmas Eve provides an opportunity to get some early preparation done for Christmas Day, while others like to start the celebrations.

COUNTDOWN

MORNING

Check that you have bought all the ingredients you will need for the next few days, as this will be your last opportunity before the shops close for two or three days.

If you prepare Poached Salmon (see page 39) early, it is an ideal recipe to serve cold either on Christmas Eve or Christmas Day.

This is a good time to get a head start on all those special little extras – Cranberry Sauce (see page 36), Orange Rum Butter (see page 42), Brandy Butter (see page 44) and Stuffed Dates (see page 50).

To be sure of well-chilled drinks over the festivities, make extra supplies of ice cubes during the day and store them in a plastic bag in the freezer.

AFTERNOON

Make Chicken Liver Pâté (see page 34) if it is on the Christmas Day or Christmas Eve menu. Make Melba toast (thinly sliced bread toasted until brown and crisp) at the same time and store it in an airtight container.

You may need to bake more than one batch of Mince Pies (see page 40), as they are so tempting when still warm.

EVENING

Hot Rum Punch (see page 47) and Mulled Ale or Wine (see page 48), provide a warm welcome for visitors. Even if you're not entertaining, a glass will put you in a festive mood while you're making last-minute preparations.

Lay the table for the Christmas meal to save time in the morning and try to leave the kitchen as tidy as possible.

TIMETABLES

Christmas Day

This requires almost military precision. The following countdown is for a 2.00 pm meal, but you can easily adjust the timing if you want to serve the meal earlier or later. The cooking time will also need to be increased if your turkey and gammon are larger than those stipulated.

COUNTDOWN

BREAKFAST
Scrambled Eggs with Smoked Salmon (see page 54) is quick, easy and special.

9.00–9.30 am Make Chestnut and Sausage Stuffing (see page 59) or Mushroom Stuffing (see page 60). Put white wine and champagne in the refrigerator to chill.

9.15 am Start the Glazed Gammon (page 66).

9.45 am Preheat the oven, and prepare and stuff the Roast Turkey (see page 62).

10.00 am Put the turkey in the oven. Preheat the oven and stuff the Roast Goose (see page 65), before cooking.

11.00 am Prepare the Vegetarian Roast (see page 69) to allow time for cooling. Start steaming the Christmas Pudding.

11.15 am Preheat the oven for the Vegetarian Roast.

11.30 am Put the Vegetarian Roast in the oven.

12.00 noon Start making the Bread Sauce (see page 62) to allow time for the milk to infuse.

12.30 pm Prepare and start cooking Perfect Roast Potatoes (see page 70). Remove the Cranberry Sauce from the refrigerator to bring to room temperature.

12.30–1.00 pm Make and serve Champagne Cocktails (see page 56). Open red wine to allow time for it to breathe.

12.45 pm Prepare the Brussels Sprouts with Chestnuts (see page 73).

1.00 pm Prepare the Glazed Parsnips (see page 74). Make the Festive Prawn Cocktail (see page 76).

1.30 pm Remove the roast from the oven, cover loosely with foil and leave to rest for about 15 minutes before carving or slicing.

2.00 pm Begin to serve Christmas starter.

Relax and make Irish Coffee (see page 78) before the big clear-up begins.

10 TIMETABLES

Boxing Day

This is traditionally a day for relaxing and you won't want to follow a strict timetable if you have been entertaining the day before. However, you may find it helpful to have a countdown for a 1.00 pm lunch or brunch.

COUNTDOWN

10.00 am Make Tipsy Cake (see page 93) to allow time for cooling and chilling. Make Fruit Compôte (see page 94) to allow time for chilling.

11.30 am Prepare the Turkey Pie (see page 84).

12.00 noon Prepare Turkey Chasseur (see page 82).

12.15 pm Preheat the oven for the Turkey Pie.

12.30 pm Put the Turkey Pie in the oven. Prepare Eggs Benedict (see page 88). Prepare Coronation Turkey (see page 87). Prepare Coleslaw (see page 90) and/or Waldorf Salad (see page 90) and wash any salad leaves and vegetables.

THE FESTIVE SEASON: PERFECT PREPARATIONS

There is always a lot to do over Christmas so it is worth doing some careful planning well in advance. Make a list of the food that you intend to serve, but don't be too ambitious or you'll end up exhausted and won't enjoy yourself. The recipes in this chapter can be cooked in advance, taking some of the stress out of festive entertaining.

Both Christmas Pudding (see page 14) and Christmas Cake (see page 17) can be made in November or even earlier, as they taste better if given time to mature. In any case, you will need to allow time for decorating the cake so the baking really shouldn't be left to the last minute. Some of the other Christmas goodies, such as the traditional Yule Log (see page 18), must be made closer to the day – perhaps in the week leading up to Christmas.

Busy mothers will be well aware that this is also the season for parties and Christmas fairs at school. Some of the recipes in this chapter, such as Gingerbread Figures (see page 21) and Iced Stars (see page 24), are perfect for such events because they are quick and easy to make.

Christmas pudding

 very easy   45 minutes    9 hours (6 hrs plus 3 hrs)   serves 8

INGREDIENTS

butter, for greasing
115 g/4 oz self-raising flour
1/2 tsp freshly grated nutmeg
1/2 tsp ground cloves
1/2 tsp ground cinnamon
1/2 tsp salt
175 g/6 oz shredded suet
175 g/6 oz fresh
  white breadcrumbs
450 g/1 lb raisins
225 g/8 oz sultanas
225 g/8 oz currants
25 g/1 oz flaked almonds
25 g/1 oz glacé cherries, chopped
55 g/2 oz chopped mixed peel
1 cooking apple, peeled, cored
  and grated
finely grated rind and juice of
  1/2 orange
finely grated rind and juice of
  1/2 lemon
5 tbsp stout or beer
3 eggs, lightly beaten

TO SERVE

50 ml/2 fl oz brandy
Orange Rum Butter (see page 42)
  or Brandy Butter (see page 44)
double cream

Grease a 1.7-litre/3-pint pudding basin. Cut out a large round of greaseproof paper and a large round of foil. Lay the two sheets together, butter the greaseproof paper and, holding them together, fold a pleat in the centre of the rounds to allow room for the pudding to rise during steaming.

Sift the flour, spices and salt together into a large bowl and stir in the suet, breadcrumbs, dried fruit, almonds, cherries, mixed peel, apple, orange and lemon rind. Mix together the stout or beer, orange and lemon juice and eggs, then stir into the dry ingredients. Mix thoroughly, then spoon into the basin. Cover with the pleated rounds, greaseproof side down, and tie securely with string. Place the basin in a saucepan; pour in enough boiling water to come halfway up the side of the basin and steam the pudding for 6 hours, adding more boiling water as necessary. Do not allow the saucepan to boil dry.

Leave to cool, then remove the cover and replace with fresh greaseproof and foil rounds. Store the pudding in its basin in a cool place until required.

To serve, steam the pudding for a further 3 hours. Uncover the top and run a knife blade around the inside of the basin, then turn out on to a warm dish. Gently heat the brandy in a ladle, then pour over the pudding and ignite. Serve with the orange rum butter or brandy butter and cream.

Christmas cake

 easy   30 minutes, plus icing, decorating and drying   about 3¹/₂ hours    makes 1 x 20-cm/8-inch cake

INGREDIENTS

225 g/8 oz unsalted butter, plus extra for greasing

175 g/6 oz soft brown sugar

4 eggs

225 g/8 oz plain flour

1 tsp mixed spice

¹/₂ tsp ground cinnamon

pinch of freshly grated nutmeg

pinch of salt

2 tbsp brandy, plus extra for feeding

grated rind of 1 lemon

225 g/8 oz sultanas

225 g/8 oz currants

225 g/8 oz raisins

115 g/4 oz chopped mixed peel

55 g/2 oz glacé cherries, coarsely chopped

55 g/2 oz blanched almonds, finely chopped

TO DECORATE

200 g/7 oz apricot jam

550 g/1¹/₄ lb marzipan

3 egg whites

700 g/1 lb 9 oz icing sugar, sifted

1 tbsp lemon juice

Christmas figures, holly leaves, edible silver balls, ribbon, cake frill, etc.

Grease and line a 20-cm/8-inch round cake tin. Preheat the oven to 150°C/300°F/Gas Mark 2.

Cream the butter and sugar together until light and fluffy. Beat in the eggs, one at a time, alternating with 1 tablespoon flour. Sift the remaining flour, spices and salt together into the bowl and fold in. Gently mix in the brandy. Mix together the lemon rind, dried fruit, peel, cherries and almonds and fold in. Spoon the mixture into the prepared tin and level the surface. Wrap several layers of newspaper around the outside of the tin and bake the cake for about 3¹/₂ hours, until a skewer inserted into the centre comes out clean.

Place the cake, still in the tin, on a wire rack to cool, then turn out. If you like, before storing, pierce the cake several times on the base with a cocktail stick and pour 2–3 tablespoons brandy over it. Store, wrapped up in a cool place.

To decorate, heat the jam with 2–3 tablespoons water, stirring occasionally, until melted. Pass through a sieve into a clean saucepan and bring to the boil. Simmer until the mixture reaches a coating consistency. Leave to cool, then brush the top and side of the cake with the glaze. Roll out the marzipan and use to cover the top and side of the cake smoothly. Store, uncovered, for at least 24 hours before icing.

To ice the cake, beat the egg whites until frothy, then gradually beat in half the icing sugar with a wooden spoon. Beat in the lemon juice and half the remaining sugar. Gradually beat in enough of the remaining sugar to form soft peaks. Cover and leave to stand to allow air bubbles to escape, then coat the cake with the icing using a palette knife. Raise into small peaks and decorate to taste. Leave to set in a cool place.

Yule log

 easy    35 minutes, plus icing and decorating   15 minutes   serves 8

INGREDIENTS

butter, for greasing
115 g/4 oz plain flour,
  plus extra for dusting
150 g/5 oz caster sugar, plus
  extra for sprinkling
4 eggs, separated
1 tsp almond essence
280 g/10 oz plain chocolate,
  broken into squares
225 ml/8 fl oz double cream
2 tbsp rum
icing sugar, for dusting

Preheat the oven to 190°C/375°F/Gas Mark 5. Grease and line a 40 x 28-cm/16 x 11-inch Swiss roll tin and dust with flour.

Reserve 2 tablespoons of the sugar and whisk the remainder with the egg yolks until thick and pale. Stir in the almond essence. Whisk the egg white in a clean, grease-free bowl until soft peaks form. Gradually whisk in the reserved sugar until stiff and glossy. Sift half the flour over the egg yolk mixture and fold in, then fold in one-quarter of the egg whites. Sift and fold in the remaining flour, followed by the remaining egg whites. Spoon the mixture into the tin, spreading it out evenly with a palette knife. Bake for about 15 minutes, until light golden.

Sprinkle caster sugar over a sheet of greaseproof paper and turn out the cake on to the paper. Roll up and leave to cool.

Place the chocolate in a heatproof bowl. Bring the cream to boiling point in a small saucepan, then pour over the chocolate and stir until it has melted. Beat with an electric mixer until smooth and thick. Reserve about one-third of the chocolate mixture and stir the rum into the remainder.

Unroll the cake and spread the chocolate and rum mixture over it. Re-roll and cut off a small piece diagonally at one end and arrange a piece on the side to represent a branch. Place the cake on a plate. Spread the reserved chocolate mixture evenly over the top and sides. Draw the prongs of a fork along the coating to resemble bark. Store in a cool place or the refrigerator until required. Just before serving, decorate with a sprig of holly and sift a little icing sugar over the log to represent snow.

Gingerbread figures

 very easy    30 minutes, plus 30 minutes chilling, cooling and setting   12 minutes   makes 12

INGREDIENTS

115 g/4 oz plain flour, plus
  extra for dusting
1/2 tsp ground ginger
1/2 tsp ground cinnamon
1/2 tsp bicarbonate of soda
25 g/1 oz unsalted butter, plus
  extra for greasing
2 tbsp golden syrup
55 g/2 oz soft brown sugar
1–2 tsp milk (if necessary)

GLACÉ ICING
55 g/2 oz icing sugar, sifted
1–2 tsp lukewarm water
few drops of food
  colouring (optional)
edible coloured balls

Sift the flour, ginger, cinnamon and bicarbonate of soda together into a bowl. Heat the butter, syrup and sugar in a small saucepan over a low heat, stirring occasionally, until melted and combined. Remove from the heat and leave to cool slightly, then add to the flour mixture and mix to a firm dough, adding milk if necessary. Form into a ball, wrap in clingfilm and chill for 30 minutes.

Preheat the oven to 160°C/325°F/ Gas Mark 3. Grease 2 baking sheets. Roll out the dough on a lightly floured surface to 5 mm/1/4 inch thick and stamp out figures with a gingerbread cutter. Place the figures on the baking sheets and bake for about 12 minutes, until just firm. Using a palette knife, carefully transfer to wire racks to cool.

To make the glacé icing, sift the sugar into a bowl and gradually stir in enough water to give a consistency that will coat the back of the spoon. Add a few drops of food colouring if you choose. Spoon the icing into a piping bag fitted with a fine, plain nozzle. Pipe eyes, noses and mouths and decorate the figures with buttons and edgings. Leave to set, then store in an airtight container. Press some coloured balls into the icing for eyes, nose, and buttons.

Brandy snaps

 very easy   15 minutes, plus cooling and setting   2½ hours   Makes 36

INGREDIENTS

oil, for greasing
115 g/4 oz unsalted butter
140 g/5 oz golden syrup
115 g/4 oz demerara sugar
115 g/4 oz plain flour
2 tsp ground ginger
600 ml/1 pint stiffly whipped
  double cream, to serve

Preheat the oven to 160°C/325°F/Gas Mark 3. Brush a non-stick baking sheet with oil. Place the butter, syrup and sugar in a saucepan and set over a low heat, stirring occasionally, until melted and combined. Remove the saucepan from the heat and leave to cool slightly. Sift the flour and ground ginger together into the butter mixture and beat until smooth. Spoon 2 teaspoons of the mixture on to the baking sheet, spacing them well apart. Bake for 8 minutes, until pale golden brown. Keep the remaining mixture warm. Meanwhile, oil the handle of a wooden spoon.

Remove the baking sheet from the oven and leave to stand for 1 minute so the brandy snaps firm up slightly. Remove one with a palette knife and immediately curl it around the handle of the wooden spoon. Once set, carefully slide off the handle and transfer to a wire rack to cool completely.

Repeat with the other brandy snap. On a cool baking sheet, bake the remaining mixture and shape in the same way. Do not be tempted to cook more than 2 brandy snaps at a time or the rounds will set before you have time to shape them. When all the brandy snaps are cool, store in an airtight container.

To serve, spoon the double cream into a piping bag fitted with a star nozzle. Fill the brandy snaps with cream from both ends.

$\mathcal{I}$ced stars

 extremely easy
 30 minutes plus chilling, cooling and setting
 8–10 minutes
 Makes 30–36

INGREDIENTS

175 g/6 oz unsalted butter
300 g/10½ oz vanilla sugar
1 egg, plus 1 egg yolk
grated rind of ½ orange
300 g/10½ oz plain flour, plus extra for dusting
pinch of salt
4 x quantity Glacé Icing (see page 21)
edible silver balls

Cream together the butter and vanilla sugar until light and fluffy. Gradually mix in the egg, egg yolk and orange rind. Sift the flour and salt together over the mixture and fold in to make a dough. Gather the dough into a ball, wrap in clingfilm and chill for 30 minutes.

Preheat the oven to 190°C/ 375°F/Gas Mark 5. Roll out the dough on a lightly floured surface to 3–5 mm/⅛–¼ inch thick. Stamp out shapes with a lightly floured star cutter and place on 2 non-stick baking sheets. Gather up and re-roll the trimmings to make more stars. Bake for 8–10 minutes, until light golden brown. Transfer to a wire rack to cool completely.

When cold, spread the glacé icing over the stars and arrange the silver balls in a decorative pattern on top. Leave to set, then store in an airtight container.

Chocolate truffles

 extremely easy 15 minutes, plus setting 5 minutes Makes 18

INGREDIENTS

125 g/4¹/₂ oz plain chocolate, broken into pieces
2 tbsp brandy, rum or whisky
40 g/1¹/₂ oz unsalted butter, diced
55 g/2 oz icing sugar, sifted
55 g/2 oz ground almonds
cocoa powder, for dusting

Place the chocolate in a heatproof bowl and melt over a saucepan of barely simmering water. Do not allow the base of the bowl to touch the surface of the water. Remove from the heat, stir in the brandy, rum or whisky and leave to cool slightly. Beat in the butter, sugar and almonds until thoroughly combined. Shape the mixture into 18 small balls and place on a sheet of baking paper.

Sift the cocoa powder into a shallow dish or on to a plate. Roll each of the balls in the cocoa to coat, shake off the excess and leave on the baking paper until set. Store in an airtight container, interleaving the layers with baking paper.

Sloe gin

 extremely easy

 25 minutes, plus 3 months standing

 none

 makes about 700 ml/1¹/₄ pints

INGREDIENTS

350 g/12 oz sloes
175/6 oz caster sugar
700 ml/1¹/₂ pints gin

Rinse the sloes thoroughly and remove the stalks. Prick them all over with a cocktail stick. Pack the sloes into a sterilized preserving jar, sprinkling each layer with sugar. Pour in the gin and seal the jar. Store in a cool, dark place for 3 months, shaking the jar occasionally.

Strain the gin into a jug, then pour into a sterilized bottle, seal and label. The sloe gin will be ready for drinking, but may be stored for up to 1 year – next Christmas in fact.

Cheese straws

 very easy 30 minutes 10 minutes serves 10–12

INGREDIENTS

115 g/4 oz unsalted butter, plus
  extra for greasing
115 g/4 oz plain flour, plus
  extra for dusting
pinch of salt
pinch of paprika
1 tsp mustard powder
85 g/3 oz grated cheese, such
  as Cheddar or Gruyère
1 egg, lightly beaten
1–2 tbsp cold water
poppy seeds, for sprinkling

Preheat the oven to 200°C/400°F/Gas Mark 6. Lightly grease 2 baking sheets with butter.

Sift the flour, salt, paprika and mustard powder into a bowl. Add the butter, cut it into the flour with a knife, then rub in with your fingertips until the mixture resembles breadcrumbs. Stir in the cheese and add about half the beaten egg. Then mix in enough water to make a firm dough. The dough may be stored in the freezer. Thaw at room temperature before rolling out.

Spread out the poppy seeds on a shallow plate. Turn the dough on to a lightly floured surface and knead briefly, then roll out. Using a sharp knife, cut the dough into strips measuring about 10 x 0.5 cm/ 4 x $1/4$ inch. Brush with the remaining beaten egg and roll some or all of the straws in the poppy seeds to coat, then arrange them on the baking sheets. Gather up the dough trimmings and re-roll. Stamp out 10–12 rounds with a 6-cm/$2^1/_2$-inch fluted cutter, then stamp out the centres with a 5-cm/2-inch plain cutter. Brush with beaten egg and place on the baking sheets.

Bake for about 10 minutes, until golden brown. Leave the cheese straws on the baking sheets to cool slightly, then transfer to wire racks to cool completely. Store in an airtight container. Thread the pastry straws through the pastry rings before serving.

CHRISTMAS EVE: THE FINAL COUNTDOWN

Christmas morning is bound to be a busy time for the family cook so anything that can be done the day before will save valuable time. The recipes in this chapter include many extras that make all the difference to the Christmas meal but there is seldom enough time to make them on the day. Home-made Cranberry Sauce (see page 36) and Brandy Butter (see page 44), for example, are much tastier than their ready-made counterparts and are quick and easy to make in advance and store overnight in the refrigerator.

Chicken Liver Pâté (see page 34) is always a popular starter and this, too, can be made the day before. Poached Salmon (see page 39) is ideal for a Christmas evening buffet as it looks wonderful and is a pleasant contrast to the roast turkey or goose eaten earlier in the day. Prepare it on Christmas Eve to avoid having to spend any extra time in the kitchen on Christmas Day. Gluttons for punishment who intend to entertain on Christmas Eve as well as Christmas Day will also find both these recipes ideal for a festive Christmas Eve menu. For a more informal gathering, you might offer Hot Rum Punch (see page 47) and warm Mince Pies (see page 40).

Chicken liver pâté

 extremely easy

 20 minutes, plus cooling and chilling

 8 minutes

 serves 4–6

INGREDIENTS

200 g/7 oz butter

225 g/8 oz trimmed chicken livers, thawed if frozen

2 tbsp Marsala or brandy

1$^{1}/_{2}$ tsp chopped fresh sage

1 garlic clove, coarsely chopped

150 ml/$^{1}/_{4}$ pint double cream

salt and pepper

fresh bay leaves or sage leaves, to garnish

Melba toast, to serve

Melt 40 g/1$^{1}/_{2}$ oz of the butter in a large, heavy-based frying pan. Add the chicken livers and cook over a medium heat for about 4 minutes on each side. They should be browned on the outside but still pink in the middle. Transfer to a food processor and process until finely chopped.

Stir the Marsala or brandy into the pan, scraping up any sediment with a wooden spoon, then add to the food processor with the chopped sage, garlic and 100 g/3$^{1}/_{2}$ oz of the remaining butter. Process until smooth. Add the cream, season with salt and pepper and process until thoroughly combined and smooth. Spoon the pâté into a dish or individual ramekins, smooth the surface and leave to cool completely.

Melt the remaining butter, then spoon it over the surface of the pâté. Decorate with herb leaves, cool, then chill in the refrigerator. Serve with Melba toast.

Cranberry sauce

 extremely easy

 10 minutes

 10–12 minutes

 serves 8

INGREDIENTS

thinly pared rind and juice
  of 1 lemon

thinly pared rind and juice
  of 1 orange

350 g/12 oz cranberries, thawed
  if frozen

140 g/5 oz caster sugar

2 tbsp arrowroot mixed with
  3 tbsp cold water

Cut strips of lemon and orange rind into thin shreds and place in a heavy-based saucepan. If using fresh cranberries, rinse well and remove any stalks. Add the berries, citrus juice and sugar and cook over a medium heat, stirring occasionally, for about 5 minutes, until the berries begin to burst.

Strain the juice into a clean saucepan and reserve the cranberries. Stir the arrowroot mixture into the juice, then bring to the boil, stirring constantly, until the sauce is smooth and thickened. Remove from the heat and stir in the reserved cranberries.

Transfer the cranberry sauce to a bowl and leave to cool, then cover with clingfilm and chill in the refrigerator.

Poached salmon

INGREDIENTS

4 litres/7 pints water
6 tbsp white wine vinegar
1 large onion, sliced
2 carrots, sliced
1¹/₂ tbsp salt
1 tsp black peppercorns
1 x 2.7-kg/6-lb salmon, cleaned, with gills and eyes removed

TO SERVE
mixed salad leaves
1 cucumber, thinly sliced
1 pimiento-stuffed olive
lemon wedges
Mayonnaise (see page 90), already prepared

To make the stock (court-bouillon) in which to poach the fish, put the water, vinegar, onion, carrots, salt and peppercorns in a large fish kettle, or covered roasting tin, and bring to the boil. Lower the heat and simmer for 20 minutes. Remove the trivet (if using the fish kettle) and lay the salmon on it. Lower it into the court-bouillon, cover, bring back to simmering point and cook for 5 minutes. Turn off the heat and leave the fish, covered, to cool in the liquid.

When the fish is cold, lift it out of the kettle on the trivet and drain well. Using 2 fish slices, carefully transfer to a board. Using a sharp knife, slit the skin along the backbone and around the back of the head, then peel off. Carefully turn the fish over and peel off the skin on the other side.

To serve, line a serving platter with green salad leaves and carefully transfer the salmon to the platter. Arrange the cucumber slices decoratively over part or all of the fish. Halve the olive and place a half in the exposed eye socket. Garnish with lemon wedges and serve with a bowl of mayonnaise.

Mince pies

 easy 20 minutes, plus chilling 20 minutes makes 18–20

INGREDIENTS

350 g/12 oz plain flour, plus
  extra for dusting
175 g/6 oz butter, at room
  temperature
85 g/3 oz caster sugar, plus
  extra for sprinkling
2 egg yolks
1–2 drops vanilla essence
450 g/1 lb mincemeat

Sift the flour on to a work surface or board and make a well in the centre. Place the butter, sugar, egg yolks and vanilla essence in the well and mix together with your fingertips. Very gradually work in the flour with your fingertips until it is fully incorporated. If the pastry seems too crumbly, add a small amount of iced water. Shape into a ball, wrap in clingfilm and chill for 30 minutes.

Preheat the oven to 190°C/375°F/Gas Mark 5. Divide the pastry in half. Roll out one piece on a lightly floured surface and stamp out 18–20 rounds with a 7.5-cm/3-inch fluted cutter. Use these to line deep tartlet tins. Using a teaspoon, divide the mincemeat among them. Do not overfill; they should be about two-thirds full. Roll out the second piece of pastry and stamp out 18–20 rounds with a 6-cm/ 2^1/$_2$-inch fluted cutter. Cover the pies with the smaller pastry rounds, sealing the edges well. Make 2 small slits in each lid. If you like, roll out the dough trimmings, cut out small holly leaves, brush with water and use to decorate the tops of the pies. Bake for 20 minutes, until golden brown.

Using a palette knife, transfer the pies to a cooling rack and sprinkle with caster sugar. Serve warm or at room temperature.

Orange rum butter

INGREDIENTS

115 g/4 oz unsalted butter, at
  room temperature
115 g/4 oz soft light brown sugar
finely grated rind of 1 orange
pinch of mixed spice
3 tbsp rum

Cream the butter in a bowl until it is very smooth and soft. Gradually beat in the sugar, orange rind and mixed spice. Add the rum, a little at a time, beating well after each addition and taking care not to let the mixture curdle.

Spoon the orange rum butter into a small serving dish, cover with clingfilm and chill until required.

Brandy butter

 extremely easy   15 minutes, plus chilling   none   serves 6–8

INGREDIENTS

115 g/4 oz unsalted butter,
 at room temperature
55 g/2 oz caster sugar
55 g/2 oz icing sugar, sifted
3 tbsp brandy

Cream the butter in a bowl until it is very smooth and soft. Gradually beat in both types of sugar. Add the brandy, a little at a time, beating well after each addition and taking care not to let the mixture curdle.

Spread out the butter on a sheet of foil and chill until firm. Stamp out decorative shapes with tiny cutters and place on a baking sheet or flat tray. Cover and chill until required.

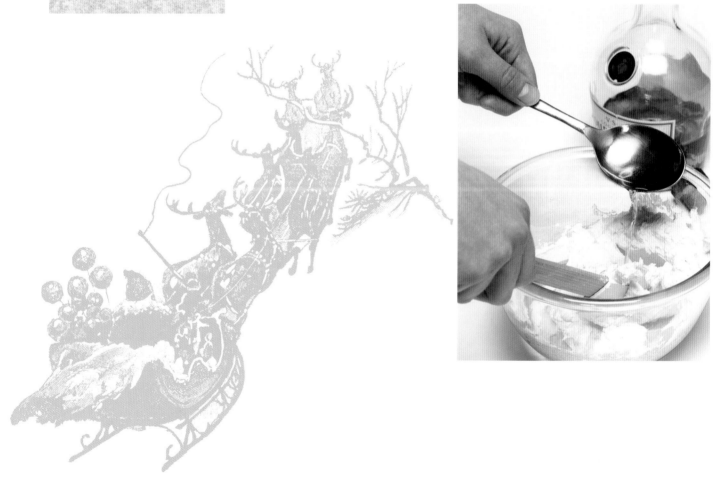

Hot rum punch

 extremely easy   15 minutes   none  makes 4 litres/7 pints

INGREDIENTS

850 ml/1½ pints rum
850 ml/1½ pints brandy
600 ml/1 pint freshly squeezed lemon juice
3–4 tbsp caster sugar
2 litres/3½ pints boiling water
orange and lemon slices, to decorate

Mix together the rum, brandy, lemon juice and 3 tablespoons of the sugar in a punch bowl or large mixing bowl. Pour in the boiling water and stir well to mix. Taste and add more sugar if required. Decorate with the fruit slices and serve immediately in heatproof glasses.

Mulled ale and Mulled wine

MULLED ALE INGREDIENTS

2.5 litres/4^1/$_2$ pints strong ale
300 ml/^{1}/$_2$ pint brandy
2 tbsp caster sugar
large pinch of ground cloves
large pinch of ground ginger

MULLED WINE INGREDIENTS

5 oranges
50 cloves
thinly pared rind and juice of
  4 lemons
850 ml/1^1/$_2$ pints water
115 g/4 oz caster sugar
2 cinnamon sticks
2 litres/3^1/$_2$ pints red wine
150 ml/^{1}/$_4$ pint brandy

Mulled ale

 extremely easy   5 minutes   5–8 minutes   makes 2.8 litres / 5 pints

Put all the ingredients in a heavy-based saucepan and heat gently, stirring until the sugar has dissolved. Continue to heat so that it is simmering but not boiling. Remove the pan from the heat and serve the ale immediately in heatproof glasses.

Mulled wine

 extremely easy    15 minutes, plus 10 minutes standing   10–15 minutes   makes about 3.6 litres / 5^3/$_4$ pints

Prick the skins of 3 of the oranges all over with a fork and stud with the cloves, then set aside. Thinly pare the rind and squeeze the juice from the remaining oranges.

Put the orange rind and juice, lemon rind and juice, water, sugar and cinnamon in a heavy-based saucepan and bring to the boil over a medium heat, stirring occasionally until the sugar has dissolved. Boil for 2 minutes without stirring, then remove from the heat, stir once and leave to stand for 10 minutes. Strain the liquid into a heatproof jug, pressing down on the contents of the sieve to extract all the juice.

Pour the wine into another saucepan and add the strained spiced juices, the brandy and clove-studded oranges. Simmer gently without boiling, then remove the pan from the heat. Strain into heatproof glasses and serve the wine immediately.

Stuffed dates

 extremely easy   20 minutes   none   serves 6–8

INGREDIENTS

500 g/1 lb 2 oz fresh dates
275 g/9¹/₂ oz marzipan

Using a small, sharp knife, cut lengthways along the side of each date and carefully remove the stones. Divide the marzipan into the same number of pieces as there are dates and roll each piece into a long oval. Insert a marzipan oval into each date and press lightly together.

Place the stuffed dates in petit four cases and store in an airtight container in the refrigerator until about 30 minutes before they are required. Bring to room temperature before serving.

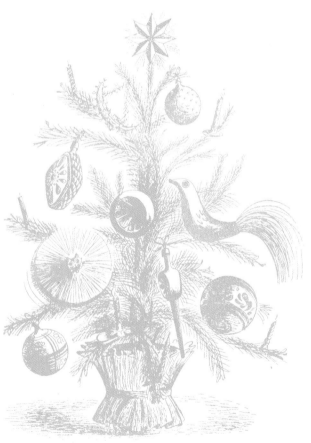

CHRISTMAS DAY: THE HIGHLIGHT OF THE CELEBRATIONS

Christmas dinner is hard work, but it's worth it as it is the focal point of the family celebrations. The recipes in this chapter provide fail-safe guidance for cooking all the traditional favourites from Roast Turkey (see page 62) to Brussels Sprouts with Chestnuts (see page 73).

Start the day on a festive note with Scrambled Eggs with Smoked Salmon (see page 54) and, if you really want to push the boat out, serve them with Buck's Fizz, one of the Champagne Cocktails (see page 56). However, you might prefer to delay the cocktails until the roast is safely in the oven and your guests have arrived.

There is a wide choice of special dishes for Christmas Day, including a Vegetarian Roast (see page 69) and two different kinds of stuffing (see pages 59 and 60), both of which are suitable for turkey and goose. The Festive Prawn Cocktail (see page 76) makes a tempting starter that can be prepared quickly and easily in the morning. Don't forget to steam the Christmas pudding on Christmas morning.

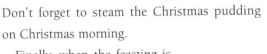

Finally, when the feasting is over and before you even contemplate cleaning up in the kitchen, treat yourself and your guests to a glass of Irish Coffee (see page 78).

Scrambled eggs with smoked salmon

 very easy 10 minutes 5 minutes serves 4

INGREDIENTS

115 g/4 oz smoked salmon slices
6 large eggs
3 tbsp single cream
40 g/1¹/2 oz butter
salt and pepper
2 slices of toast, buttered and
  cut into 8 triangles, to serve

Using a sharp knife, chop the smoked salmon. Lightly beat the eggs with the cream until just combined.

Melt the butter in a heavy-based saucepan over a low heat. When it begins to foam, pour in the egg mixture and cook, stirring constantly, until creamy and just beginning to set. Turn off the heat and stir in the smoked salmon. Remove the saucepan from the hob and season the scrambled eggs with salt and pepper to taste, remembering that the fish will be quite salty.

Divide the scrambled egg mixture between warm plates and serve immediately with the toast triangles.

Champagne cocktails

 extremely easy   2 minutes each    none   each recipe serves 1

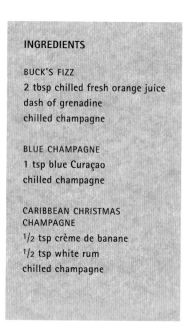

INGREDIENTS

BUCK'S FIZZ
2 tbsp chilled fresh orange juice
dash of grenadine
chilled champagne

BLUE CHAMPAGNE
1 tsp blue Curaçao
chilled champagne

CARIBBEAN CHRISTMAS
CHAMPAGNE
1/2 tsp crème de banane
1/2 tsp white rum
chilled champagne

For the buck's fizz, pour the orange juice into a chilled champagne flute, add a dash of grenadine and stir well. Top up with chilled champagne and serve immediately.

For the blue champagne, pour the Curaçao into a chilled champagne flute and swirl to coat the sides of the glass. Fill with chilled champagne and serve immediately.

For the Caribbean Christmas champagne, pour the crème de banane and rum into a chilled champagne flute. Fill with chilled champagne and stir gently. Serve immediately.

Chestnut and sausage stuffing

 extremely easy   15 minutes   30–40 minutes   serves 6-8

INGREDIENTS

225 g/8 oz pork sausagemeat

225 g/8 oz unsweetened chestnut purée

85 g/3 oz walnuts, chopped

115 g/4 oz ready-to-eat dried apricots, chopped

2 tbsp chopped fresh parsley

2 tbsp chopped fresh chives

2 tsp chopped fresh sage

4–5 tbsp double cream

salt and pepper

Combine the sausagemeat and chestnut purée in a bowl, then stir in the walnuts, apricots, parsley, chives and sage. Stir in enough double cream to make a firm, but not dry, mixture. Season with salt and pepper.

If you are planning to stuff a turkey or goose, fill only the neck cavity. It is safer and more reliable to cook the stuffing separately, either rolled into small balls and placed on a baking sheet or spooned into an ovenproof dish.

Cook the separate stuffing in an oven for 30–40 minutes at 190°C/ 375°F/Gas Mark 5. It should be allowed a longer time if you are roasting a bird at a lower temperature in the same oven.

Mushroom stuffing

  extremely easy 10 minutes 40–50 minutes  serves 6–8

INGREDIENTS

55 g/2 oz butter
3 shallots, chopped
225 g/8 oz mixed wild and
  cultivated mushrooms, chopped
115 g/4 oz pork sausagemeat
85 g/3 oz fresh white
  breadcrumbs
few drops of truffle oil (optional)
salt and pepper

Melt the butter in a heavy-based frying pan over a low heat. Add the shallots and cook, stirring occasionally, for about 5 minutes, until softened. Add the mushrooms and cook, stirring occasionally, until their juices have evaporated. Transfer the mixture to a bowl and stir in the sausagemeat, breadcrumbs and truffle oil, if you like, and season to taste with salt and pepper.

If you are planning to stuff a turkey or goose, fill only the neck cavity. It is safer and more reliable to cook the stuffing separately, either rolled into small balls and placed on a baking sheet or spooned into an ovenproof dish.

Cook the separate stuffing in an oven for 30–40 minutes at 190°C/ 375°F/Gas Mark 5. It should be allowed a longer time if you are roasting a bird at a lower temperature in the same oven.

Roast turkey with bread sauce

 very easy   20 minutes   3½ hours   serves 8

INGREDIENTS

1 quantity Chestnut and Sausage
   Stuffing (see page 59)
   or Mushroom Stuffing
   (see page 60)
1 x 5-kg/11-lb turkey
55 g/2 oz butter
5 tbsp red wine
400 ml/14 fl oz chicken stock,
   bought fresh or made with a
   stock cube
1 tbsp cornflour
1 tsp French mustard
1 tsp sherry vinegar

BREAD SAUCE
1 onion, peeled
4 cloves
600 ml/1 pint milk
115 g/4 oz fresh white
   breadcrumbs
55 g/2 oz butter
salt and pepper

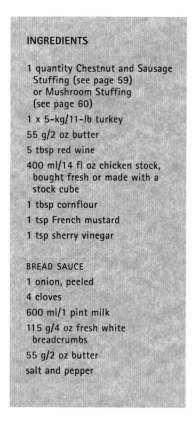

Preheat the oven to 220°C/425°F/Gas Mark 7. Spoon the stuffing into the neck cavity of the turkey and close the flap of skin with a skewer. Place the bird in a large roasting tin and rub all over with 40 g/1½ oz of the butter. Roast for 1 hour, then lower the oven temperature to 180°C/350°F/Gas Mark 4 and roast for a further 2½ hours. You may need to pour off the fat from the roasting tin occasionally.

Meanwhile, make the bread sauce. Stud the onion with the cloves, then place in a saucepan with the milk, breadcrumbs and butter. Bring just to boiling point over a low heat, then remove from the heat and leave to stand in a warm place to infuse. Just before serving, remove the onion and reheat the sauce gently, beating well with a wooden spoon. Season to taste with salt and pepper.

Check that the turkey is cooked by inserting a skewer or the point of a sharp knife into the thigh; if the juices run clear, it is ready. Transfer the bird to a carving board, cover loosely with foil and leave to rest.

To make the gravy, skim off the fat from the roasting tin then place the tin over a medium heat. Add the red wine and stir with a wooden spoon, scraping up the sediment from the base of the tin. Stir in the chicken stock. Mix the cornflour, mustard, vinegar and 2 teaspoons water together in a small bowl, then stir into the wine and stock. Bring to the boil, stirring constantly until thickened and smooth. Stir in the remaining butter.

Carve the turkey and serve with the warm bread sauce and all the trimmings – including stuffing, potatoes and gravy.

Roast goose

  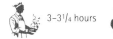

very easy   15 minutes   3–3¼ hours   serves 8

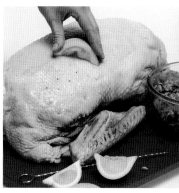 

INGREDIENTS

1 x 4-kg/9-lb goose

1 lemon, cut into quarters

1 quantity Chestnut and Sausage Stuffing (see page 59) or Mushroom Stuffing (see page 60)

5 tbsp medium sherry

400 ml/14 fl oz chicken stock bought fresh or made with a stock cube

1 tbsp cornflour

1 tsp Dijon mustard

1 tsp red wine vinegar

15 g/½ oz butter

salt and pepper

Preheat the oven to 230°C/450°F/Gas Mark 8. Prick the skin of the goose all over with a fine skewer or fork. Rub with 3 of the lemon quarters and season with salt and pepper. Squeeze the juice from the remaining lemon quarter into the cavity. Spoon the stuffing into the neck cavity of the bird and fasten the flap of skin with a skewer.

Place the goose, breast side down, on a wire rack set over a roasting tin and roast for 15 minutes. Reduce the oven temperature to 180°C/350°F/Gas Mark 4 and roast for a further 2¾–3 hours. Halfway through the cooking time, turn the goose on to its back. You may need to pour off the fat from the roasting tin occasionally. Save it for making perfect roast potatoes today or on another day (see page 70).

Check that the goose is cooked by inserting a skewer or the point of a sharp knife into the thigh; if the juices run clear, it is ready. Transfer the bird to a carving board, cover loosely with foil and leave to rest.

To make the gravy, skim off the fat from the roasting tin then place the tin over a medium heat. Add the sherry and stir with a wooden spoon, scraping up the sediment from the base of the tin. Stir in the chicken stock. Mix together the cornflour, mustard, vinegar and 2 teaspoons water in a small bowl, then stir into the wine and stock. Bring to the boil, stirring constantly until thickened and smooth. Whisk in the butter.

Carve the goose and serve with all the trimmings – including the stuffing, potatoes and gravy.

Glazed gammon

 very easy    20 minutes   4¹/₄ hours   serves 8

INGREDIENTS

1 x 4-kg/9-lb gammon joint
1 apple, cored and chopped
1 onion, chopped
300 ml/¹/₂ pint cider
6 black peppercorns
1 bouquet garni
bay leaf
about 50 cloves
4 tbsp demerara sugar

Put the gammon in a large saucepan and add enough cold water to cover. Bring to the boil and skim off the scum that rises to the surface. Reduce the heat and simmer for 30 minutes. Drain the gammon and return to the saucepan. Add the apple, onion, cider, peppercorns, bouquet garni, bay leaf and a few of the cloves. Pour in enough fresh water to cover and bring back to the boil. Cover and simmer for 3 hours 20 minutes.

Preheat the oven to 200°C/400°F/Gas Mark 6. Take the saucepan off the heat and set aside to cool slightly. Remove the gammon from the cooking liquid and, while it is still warm, loosen the rind with a sharp knife, then peel it off and discard. Score the fat into diamond shapes and stud with the remaining cloves. Place the gammon on a rack in a roasting tin and sprinkle with the sugar. Roast, basting occasionally with the cooking liquid, for 20 minutes. Serve hot, or cold later.

Vegetarian roast

 very easy   30 minutes, plus cooling and standing   1 hour 30 minutes   serves 8

INGREDIENTS

115 g/4 oz walnuts
115 g/4 oz hazelnuts
55 g/2 oz butter or vegetarian margarine
2 onions, finely chopped
1 large carrot, finely chopped
115 g/4 oz mushrooms, finely chopped
2 celery sticks, finely chopped
dash of Tabasco sauce
oil, for greasing
115 g/4 oz red lentils, soaked in water for 30 minutes and drained
2 tbsp Worcestershire sauce
2 tbsp tomato ketchup
1 egg, lightly beaten
3 tbsp chopped fresh parsley
salt
Cranberry Sauce (see page 36), to serve

Place the nuts in a food processor and grind until fairly fine, then set aside. Melt the butter or margarine in a large saucepan and add the onions, carrot, mushrooms and celery. Cook over a medium heat, stirring occasionally, for 5 minutes. Stir in the Tabasco and cook for a few seconds more. Remove the saucepan from the heat and leave to cool.

Preheat the oven to 190°C/375°F/Gas Mark 5. Grease and line a 1-kg/ 2-lb loaf tin with foil or greaseproof paper. Transfer the vegetable mixture to a large bowl and stir in the ground nuts, lentils, Worcestershire sauce, tomato ketchup, egg and parsley. Season with salt.

Spoon the mixture into the prepared tin, pressing it in firmly, and roast for 1¼ hours, until just firm to the touch. After 45 minutes, cover the surface with lightly oiled greaseproof paper.

Remove the tin from the oven and leave to stand for 15 minutes. Peel off the paper, turn out and cut into slices. Serve hot or cold with cranberry sauce.

Perfect roast potatoes

 extremely easy   10 minutes   1 hr 25 minutes   serves 8

INGREDIENTS

70 g/2¹/₂ oz goose fat or duck fat or 5 tbsp olive oil

coarse sea salt

1 kg/2 lb 4 oz even-sized potatoes, peeled

8 fresh rosemary sprigs, to garnish

Preheat the oven to 230°C/450°F/Gas Mark 8. Put the fat or oil in a large roasting tin, sprinkle generously with sea salt and place in the oven.

Meanwhile, cook the potatoes in a large pan of boiling water for 8–10 minutes, until par-boiled. Drain well, and if the potatoes are large, cut them in half. Return the potatoes to the pan and shake vigorously to roughen their outsides.

Arrange the potatoes in a single layer in the hot tin and roast for 45 minutes. If they look as if they are beginning to char around the edges, lower the oven temperature to 200°C/400°F/Gas Mark 6. Turn the potatoes over and roast for a further 30 minutes, until crisp. Serve garnished with sprigs of rosemary.

Brussels sprouts with chestnuts

 very easy 20 minutes   55 minutes serves 8

INGREDIENTS

450 g/1 lb fresh chestnuts
225 ml/8 fl oz milk
55 g/2 oz butter
1/2 small onion, finely chopped
700 g/1 lb 9 oz Brussels sprouts, trimmed with a small cross in the base

First cook the chestnuts. Bring a saucepan of water to the boil, add the chestnuts, bring back to the boil and cook for 8–10 minutes. Drain and, when cool enough to handle, peel them.

Place the peeled chestnuts in a saucepan and add the milk and enough water to cover. Bring to the boil, lower the heat and simmer for 15 minutes. Drain and set aside.

Melt the butter in a heavy-based sauté pan. Add the onion and cook over a low heat, stirring occasionally, for 5 minutes, until softened. Add the Brussels sprouts and 3 tablespoons water. Cover and cook for 8 minutes. Stir in the chestnuts, re-cover the pan and cook for a further 5 minutes or until the Brussels sprouts are tender. Transfer to a warm serving dish and serve immediately.

Glazed parsnips

  extremely easy 10 minutes 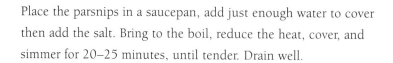 35–45 minutes serves 8

INGREDIENTS

24 small parsnips, peeled
about 1 tsp salt
115 g/4 oz butter
115 g/3 oz soft brown sugar

Place the parsnips in a saucepan, add just enough water to cover then add the salt. Bring to the boil, reduce the heat, cover, and simmer for 20–25 minutes, until tender. Drain well.

Melt the butter in a heavy pan or wok. Add the parsnips and toss well. Sprinkle with the sugar then cook, stirring frequently to prevent the sugar from sticking to the pan or burning. Cook the parsnips for 10–15 minutes, until golden and glazed. Transfer to a warm serving dish and serve immediately.

$\mathcal{F}$estive
prawn cocktail

 extremely easy   30 minutes   none   serves 8

INGREDIENTS

350 ml/12 fl oz Mayonnaise
  (see page 90), already prepared
125 ml/4 fl oz tomato ketchup
1 tsp chilli sauce
1 tsp Worcestershire sauce
1 kg/2 lb 4 oz cooked tiger
  prawns
2 ruby grapefruits
lettuce leaves, shredded
2 avocados, peeled, stoned
  and diced

TO GARNISH
lime slices
dill sprigs

Mix together the mayonnaise, tomato ketchup, chilli sauce and Worcestershire sauce in a small bowl. Cover with clingfilm and place in the refrigerator until required.

Remove the heads from the prawns and peel off the shells, leaving the tails intact. Slit along the length of the back of each prawn with a sharp knife and remove the dark vein. Cut off a slice from the top and bottom of each grapefruit, then peel off the skin and all the white pith. Cut between the membranes to separate the segments.

When ready to serve, make a bed of shredded lettuce in the base of 8 glass dishes. Divide the prawns, grapefruit segments and avocados among them and spoon over the mayonnaise dressing. Serve garnished with lime slices and dill sprigs.

*I*rish coffee

 very easy   10 minutes   5 minutes   serves 8

INGREDIENTS

8 sugar cubes
125 ml/4 fl oz water
225 ml/8 fl oz Irish whiskey
600 ml/1 pint freshly made,
  strong black coffee
225 ml/8 fl oz double cream,
  chilled

Place the sugar cubes and water in a saucepan and heat gently, stirring until the sugar has dissolved. Divide among 8 heatproof glasses. Add about 2 tablespoons whiskey to each glass, then pour in the coffee. Stir well.

Hold a teaspoon against the side of a glass with the back of the spoon facing upwards. Pour about 2 tablespoons of cream over the spoon so that it floats on top of the coffee. Repeat with the remaining glasses, then serve.

Boxing Day: Luxury Leftovers

After the hectic effort of preparing the Christmas meal the day before and the heroic clearing up afterwards, no one wants to spend much time in the kitchen the following day. Nevertheless, simply serving slices of cold turkey and ham can be something of an anticlimax. The recipes in this chapter suggest more interesting ways of serving leftovers that don't involve too much cooking and are perfect for the more informal but still festive atmosphere. You may be surprised how easily appetites can be tempted even after a sumptuous Christmas dinner, a late night and lots of excitement.

Succulent Turkey Chasseur (see page 82), Crisp Turkey Pie (see page 84) and Coronation Turkey (see page 87) are impressive dishes that are sure to be popular. Eggs Benedict (see page 88) provides the perfect opportunity to use up any leftover gammon and is ideal for a casual brunch. If you are planning to serve simple cold meats, why not brighten them up with a colourful Waldorf Salad or a crunchy home-made Coleslaw (see page 90) along with a green salad.

Finally, if you're still in the mood for self-indulgence but don't fancy cold Christmas Pudding, round off your Boxing Day feast with a rich, creamy Tipsy Cake (see page 93) or a deliciously refreshing Fruit Compôte (see page 94).

Turkey chasseur

  easy 20 minutes 35–40 minutes serves 6

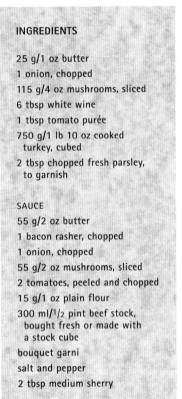

INGREDIENTS

25 g/1 oz butter
1 onion, chopped
115 g/4 oz mushrooms, sliced
6 tbsp white wine
1 tbsp tomato purée
750 g/1 lb 10 oz cooked
  turkey, cubed
2 tbsp chopped fresh parsley,
  to garnish

SAUCE
55 g/2 oz butter
1 bacon rasher, chopped
1 onion, chopped
55 g/2 oz mushrooms, sliced
2 tomatoes, peeled and chopped
15 g/1 oz plain flour
300 ml/1/2 pint beef stock,
  bought fresh or made with
  a stock cube
bouquet garni
salt and pepper
2 tbsp medium sherry

First, make the sauce. Melt the butter in a heavy-based saucepan. Add the bacon, onion, mushrooms and tomatoes and cook over a low heat, stirring occasionally, for 5 minutes. Stir in the flour and cook, stirring constantly until it begins to turn golden. Gradually stir in the stock and bring to the boil. Continue to stir until thickened and smooth. Add the bouquet garni and season with salt and pepper. Lower the heat and simmer for 15 minutes. Leave to cool slightly, then transfer to a blender or food processor and process until smooth. Stir in the sherry.

Melt the butter in a saucepan and add the onion and mushrooms. Cook over a low heat, stirring occasionally, for 5 minutes. Stir in the prepared sauce, wine and tomato purée and simmer for a further 5 minutes. Add the cubed turkey and heat through gently. Transfer to a warm serving dish, garnish with the parsley and serve immediately.

Turkey pie

 easy 25 minutes, plus chilling 45 minutes serves 6

INGREDIENTS

55 g/2 oz butter
2 tbsp plain flour
225 ml/8 fl oz chicken stock, bought fresh or made with a stock cube
3 tbsp double cream
salt and pepper
1 onion, chopped
2 carrots, sliced
2 celery sticks, chopped
55 g/2 oz mushrooms, sliced
450 g/1 lb cooked turkey, diced
55 g/2 oz frozen peas
1 egg, lightly beaten

PASTRY

225 g/8 oz plain flour, plus extra for dusting
pinch of salt
115 g/4 oz margarine
55 g/2 oz lard or white vegetable fat
1–2 tbsp iced water

First, make the pastry. Sift the flour and a pinch of salt into a bowl. Add the margarine and lard or vegetable fat and cut them into the flour, then rub in with your fingertips until the mixture resembles breadcrumbs. Mix in sufficient iced water to make a firm dough. Gather the dough into a ball, wrap in clingfilm and chill in the refrigerator for 30 minutes.

Preheat the oven to 190°C/375°F/Gas Mark 5. Melt half the butter in a saucepan, stir in the flour and cook, stirring constantly, for 1 minute. Gradually whisk in the stock and bring to the boil, whisking constantly. Simmer for 2 minutes, then stir in the cream. Season with salt and pepper and set aside.

Melt the remaining butter in a large frying pan. Add the onion and carrots and cook over a low heat, stirring occasionally, for 5 minutes. Add the celery and mushrooms and cook for a further 5 minutes, then stir in the turkey and peas. Stir the turkey mixture into the cream sauce, then transfer to a large pie dish.

Roll out the pastry on a lightly floured surface to about 3 mm/⅛ inch thick. Cut out a rectangle about 2.5 cm/1 inch larger than the dish and lay it over the filling. Crimp the edges, cut 3–4 slits in the top to allow steam to escape and brush with the beaten egg. Roll out the trimmings and cut out shapes to decorate the pie if you like. Bake the pie for 30 minutes, until golden brown. Serve immediately.

Coronation turkey

 extremely easy
 10 minutes, plus cooling
 15 minutes
 serves 6

INGREDIENTS

15 g/¹/₂ oz butter
2 shallots, chopped
1 tbsp tomato purée
1 tbsp curry paste
125 ml/4 fl oz red wine
2 tbsp lemon juice
12 tbsp apricot jam
300 ml/¹/₂ pint Mayonnaise (see page 90)
125 ml/4 fl oz double cream
salt and pepper
750 g/1 lb 10 oz cold cooked turkey, diced
green salad, to serve

Melt the butter in a small frying pan. Add the shallots and cook over a low heat, stirring occasionally, for 5 minutes, until softened. Add the tomato purée, curry paste, wine and lemon juice and simmer gently for a further 10 minutes. Stir in the apricot jam, push through a sieve and set aside to cool.

Beat the cooled mixture into the mayonnaise. Whip the cream and fold it into the mayonnaise. Season to taste with salt and pepper and stir in the diced turkey. Serve with a green salad.

*E*ggs benedict

 very easy   10 minutes   25 minutes   serves 6

INGREDIENTS

6 eggs
3 muffins
3 slices cooked gammon

HOLLANDAISE SAUCE
3 egg yolks
1 tbsp lemon juice
salt and cayenne pepper
225 g/8 oz unsalted butter, diced
ground pepper, for dusting

First, make the hollandaise sauce. Whisk together the egg yolks, lemon juice and salt and cayenne pepper in a heatproof bowl over a saucepan of barely simmering water. Add the diced butter, whisking constantly until the butter has melted. Remove from the heat and continue whisking until the sauce is thick and creamy. Keep warm over the hot water.

Meanwhile, preheat the grill. Split the muffins in half. Using a sharp knife, cut out rounds from the gammon the same size as the muffin halves. Place the gammon rounds under the grill and cook until hot and golden.

Bring a saucepan of water to the boil, then reduce the heat so that the water is barely simmering and poach the eggs, for 3–4 minutes, until the whites are just firm. Drain with a slotted spoon and trim the whites, if necessary.

Meanwhile, toast the muffin halves. Place on 6 warmed plates, top with a slice of gammon and an egg and spoon over the sauce. Add the pepper and serve immediately.

Coleslaw and Waldorf salad

Coleslaw

 extremely easy   15 minutes   none   serves 6

COLESLAW INGREDIENTS

1/2 white cabbage
2 carrots, grated
1 eating apple, cored and chopped
4 spring onions, chopped
1 red pepper, deseeded and chopped
2 celery sticks, chopped

MAYONNAISE

2 egg yolks
4 tsp lemon juice
1 tsp mustard powder
250 ml/9 fl oz sunflower oil
1–2 tbsp hot water

First make the mayonnaise. Put the egg yolks, half the lemon juice and the mustard powder in a blender or food processor and process until combined. With the motor running, gradually add the oil in a thin stream through the feeder tube, processing until it is fully incorporated. Scrape the mayonnaise into a bowl and add enough hot water to give the required consistency.

Using a sharp knife, remove the core from the cabbage and shred the leaves finely. Mix the cabbage, carrots, apple, spring onions, red pepper and celery in a serving bowl.

Stir the remaining lemon juice into the mayonnaise, then stir into the salad. Mix well and serve immediately.

Waldorf salad

 extremely easy   10 minutes   none   serves 6

WALDORF SALAD INGREDIENTS

3 eating apples, cored and chopped
3 celery sticks, chopped
85 g/3 oz walnut halves
1 tbsp lemon juice
125 ml/4 fl oz Mayonnaise (see above)
lettuce leaves, to serve

Mix together the apples, celery and walnut halves in a bowl and sprinkle with the lemon juice. Add the mayonnaise and stir gently to mix.

Line a serving dish with lettuce leaves and spoon the salad over. Serve at room temperature.

Tipsy cake

 easy   15 minutes, plus infusing and chilling   10 minutes   serves 6

INGREDIENTS

1 x 23-cm/9-inch sponge cake
4 tbsp raspberry jam
150 ml/¹/₄ pint medium sherry
225 ml/8 fl oz double cream
55 g/2 oz glacé cherries
25 g/1 oz angelica, cut into fine strips
55 g/2 oz flaked almonds

VANILLA CREAM

450 ml/16 fl oz milk
1 vanilla pod
4 egg yolks
55 g/2 oz caster sugar

First, make the vanilla cream. Place the milk and vanilla pod in a heatproof bowl set over a saucepan of simmering water and bring to just below boiling point. Remove the bowl from the heat, cover and set aside to infuse for 10 minutes. Remove the vanilla pod, wipe dry and reserve for use in another recipe. Beat the egg yolks with the sugar in another bowl until smooth and creamy, then gradually whisk in the milk. Return the mixture to the heatproof bowl and set over simmering water. Heat gently, stirring constantly, for about 5 minutes, until thickened. Remove from the heat.

Slice the cake in half horizontally, spread one half with the jam and lay the other half on top. Pour the sherry over the cake, followed by the hot vanilla cream. Leave to cool, then chill in the refrigerator.

Beat the cream until soft peaks form, then spread it over the top and sides of the cake with a spatula to cover the vanilla cream completely. Decorate with the cherries, angelica and almonds and keep in the refrigerator until required.

*F*ruit compôte

 extremely easy   10 minutes, plus chilling   20 minutes   serves 6

INGREDIENTS

350 g/12 oz raspberries
350 g/12 oz blackcurrants
85 g/3 oz caster sugar
150 ml/¹/4 pint water
2 tbsp arrowroot mixed with a little cold water
2 tbsp crème de cassis
double cream, to serve

Put the raspberries, blackcurrants, sugar and water into a heavy-based saucepan, cover and cook over a low heat for 15 minutes, until the fruit is soft.

Stir the arrowroot paste and place in a saucepan. Bring the mixture to the boil, stirring constantly until thickened. Remove from the heat and leave to cool slightly, before stirring in the blackcurrants, raspberries and the crème de cassis.

Pour the compôte into a glass bowl, leave to cool, then chill for at least 1 hour. To serve, divide the compôte between 6 decorative glass dishes, and top with a swirl of cream.

Index